The quickest and most effective way to

FIND THAT JOB in 90 Minutes

James Alexander

2000

First published in 2005 by Management Books 2000 Ltd
Forge House, Limes Road
Kemble, Cirencester
Gloucestershire, GL7 6AD, UK
Tel: 0044 (0) 1285 771441
Fax: 0044 (0) 1285 771055
E-mail: info@mb2000.com
Web: www.mb2000.com

Printed and bound in Great Britain by Digital Books Logistics of Peterborough

British Library Cataloguing in Publication Data is available

ISBN 1-85252-491-X

FIND THAT JOB

2 1 FEB 2012		

For a complete list of Management Books 2000 titles,
visit our web-site on www.mb2000.com

The original idea for the 'In Ninety Minutes' series was
presented to the publishers by Graham Willmott, author
of 'Forget Debt in Ninety Minutes'. Thanks are due to
him for suggesting what will become a major series to
help business people, entrepreneurs, managers,
supervisors and others to greatly improve their personal
performance, after just a short period of study.

Proposed titles in the 'in Ninety Minutes' series are:

Forget Debt in Ninety Minutes
Understand Accounts in Ninety Minutes
Working Together in Ninety Minutes
Presentation in Ninety Minutes
25 Management Techniques in Ninety Minutes
Supply Chain in Ninety Minutes
Practical Negotiating in Ninety Minutes
Delegate Better in Ninety Minutes
Clever Marketing in Ninety Minutes
Managing People in Ninety Minutes
Managing Your Boss in Ninety Minutes
Better Budgeting in Ninety Minutes
… other titles may be added

The series editor is James Alexander

Submissions of possible titles for this series or for management books in
general will be welcome. MB2000 are always keen to discuss possible new
works that might be added to their extensive list of books for people who
mean business.

Contents

Introduction

> **This book has been written to -**
> **help you get a job.**
> **There is no other purpose for it. Together, maybe, we can work out some ideas that will get you back to work, or out of your present job and into a better one.**
>
> **It will take about an hour and a half to read through this little book. Then you will need to read it again (probably several times!) and use the checklists to create a powerful programme to get you into a job.**
>
> **FIND THAT JOB! - in ninety minutes**

The present market for jobs is extremely depressing, but there are ways of tackling the business of finding a job, getting an interview and even better, being offered a job. You need to have something that the other candidates have not got, a **unique selling point**, to use the salesman's pitch. You need an advantage over other applicants for every job you chase. **This book will give you that advantage**. It will offer some sound advice, built up over many years. It is a no-nonsense, plainly-written and simple book. There are no frills, no complicated theories, just amazing good sense and easily used ideas.

In somewhere around an hour and a half, you can read through this book and pick up enough really useful tips to start immediately on that job search. Don't delay – get on with it now.

About the Author

You may be saying, 'What does this fellow know about interviews and writing CVs?' A good question, but one that can be answered easily.

As a trainer for many years, teaching people about the skills of managing and conducting interviews, James Alexander built up an impressive collection of ideas and techniques that are just as important for the candidate as they are for the interviewer. If you really know how to interview other people, you also know how to be a good candidate! As a writer, he also knows about the importance of really good written English and is enthusiastic about finding the clearest words to express an idea.

Presently, James is publisher and editor with Management Books 2000 Ltd, having spent many years as trainer and manager in public and private companies and as lecturer in FE and HE, before setting up his own training consultancy in the mid-1980s.

Acknowledgement

Over the years, many fascinating and useful ideas have come my way from a wide variety of fellow workers and managers, students and colleagues. Often these ideas have locked themselves in my subconscious and have emerged in this and other books. Thank you to all those people who have unwittingly supplied me with source material that I cannot actually trace or acknowledge properly.

What's in here?

The book has a number of sections, most of which are written as **checklists**. What I would suggest is that you take these checklists very seriously indeed. They are all important in your search for a decent job. Where there are pages to be filled in, fill 'em in! The time spent doing this will be repaid handsomely when you are offered interviews with companies where you would really like to work.

The greatest advantage of using this book to help with your job search is the sound advice it offers towards writing a CV for you – the **Curriculum Vitae** that will act as your shop-window, your sales pitch and your most powerful tool in getting to meet the people who offer the jobs.

Many people have been helped by the system of CV writing described in this book. You can be another! You have bought the book so make sure you use the advice and the other sensible ideas you will find. Use this advice to create a very good application form and all the necessary letters, as well as the perfect CV.

A map of the book

This chart shows exactly what the other pages contain and how they are linked together. It is a map of all the parts of the book as well as a single-page picture of the work you have to do to get a job!

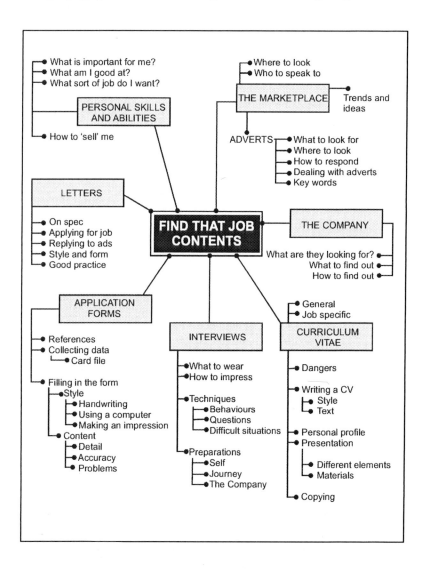

Before we start

Let us look briefly at some general principles about this business of job hunting.

 These are important points, so do not skip over these few items just because they look like a bit more of the introduction!!

> **A. Although it is <u>you</u> that the book is concerned about - you and your job search - there is still the matter of the <u>recruiter</u> to consider.**

Never lose sight of the fact that everything you do to get a job is dependent upon the recruiter agreeing that you are the ideal person for the job. The recruiter needs to fulfil certain requirements. He or she must be sure that you fit the company's specifications (all of them!); that the interview was fair from both sides; that the money spent in hiring you will be well spent.

> **B. Many people spend much of their time when hunting jobs merely being <u>applicants</u>.**
>
> ## YOU MUST BE A <u>CANDIDATE</u>!

The difference is simple – applicants are those people who apply for jobs; candidates are those people who apply for jobs but **who are also entirely suitable** in terms of experience, character and personal development.

<u>Candidates</u> get invited for interview, applicants don't!

> **C. All your activities in job-hunting are inter-linked. Every action has an importance. Every action you perform must be directed towards getting that job.**

This means that you cannot afford to be slipshod or vague, incorrect or ill-prepared. Every word you write must be the right word, heading directly towards the objective of securing the job. Every word you say in interview must be chosen to present yourself in the best light and to prove how suited you are and how well you will fit in.

> **D. You must consider yourself a very desirable property!**

When **hunting for jobs**, you must try to link up with someone who is **hunting for employees**. This means that:

- you have to be satisfied that the job or the company will be good for you

- more importantly, you have to persuade the employee hunter that you are exactly what he or she is looking for.

Be proud of your achievements so far, be sure of your worth and set out to prove to the world that you deserve a job and, by heck, you are going to get one!

The checklist of all the checklists

YOU HAVE SKILLS, ABILITIES AND TALENTS THAT OTHER PEOPLE NEED FOR THEIR SUCCESSFUL BUSINESSES.

Tell them what you are and how good you will be for them!

CHECKLIST ONE - What is important to me?

This list suggests a number of factors that could be very important to you about having a job. Choose the ten that are <u>the most important to you</u> and then look at the next page to see how these answers give you some guidance about the way you apply for work that you will find more satisfying.

PUT A MARK AGAINST THE <u>TEN</u> MOST IMPORTANT FACTORS TO YOU –

1	Having a lot of contact with people	
2	Having an important position with status	
3	Being recognised as a competent worker	
4	Communicating with others	
5	Having a real sense of purpose	
6	Being able to make decisions	
7	Working to set dates, times and deadlines	
8	Working in a team	
9	Taking some risks	
10	Having a wide variety of things to do	
11	Being creative and having new ideas	
12	Supervising the work of others	
13	Doing it my way!	
14	Finding a job with a secure future	
15	Being recognised as an expert	
16	Having work that gives me a challenge	
17	Working under pressure	
18	Having good facilities and working conditions	
19	Being fairly independent	
20	Working for a well-known organisation	
21	Not being watched all the time	
22	Not doing repetitive, routine work	
23	Opportunities for training and development	
24	Opportunities for promotion	

(As well as the factors on the previous page, we take it as read that you will also want some money for working!)

Analysing Checklist One

Once you have found the ten factors that are very important to you, try and put them into priority order. What is the most important of the ten and so on down to the tenth most important. List them in the left hand column on the following chart. Start with the most important and work downwards.

Important factors about work (most important at the top)	In present (last) job? (score out of 10)	In jobs being applied for? (scores out of 10)					
		Job A	Job B	Job C	Job D	Job E	Job F
1st							
2nd							
3rd							
4th							
5th							
6th							
7th							
8th							
9th							
10th							
Totals							

How to use this chart – it is quite simple!

In the second column, give each factor a score out of ten for how well it applies to your present (last) job. (If you have ten factors and they all score ten (totalling 100), then that job was absolutely brilliant – stay there or try to get back in!) The chances are that the score is rather less than 100! A very low score in the present (last) job column means that it is high time you left! (or a good job you did leave!).

Example

Take factor 10, for example – *having a wide variety of things to do*. Suppose that your present (last) job was rather restricting and you were only involved in a couple of really interesting things. This would score quite low, say 3 or 4.

The right-hand block gives you up to six opportunities to score jobs that you are actively pursuing, based on your assumptions about the jobs and the conditions that attach to them. Score each job in the same way – how many out of ten do you give each factor according to what you think (or know) the job will be like?

Example

One of the jobs you are looking at seems to promise a great deal of variety. This would score quite high, say 8 or 9, against factor 10 on the chart on page 15.

Ideally, you will make more effort for jobs that score highly on this chart than jobs with poor scores. Take particular note of the factors at the top of your list when comparing jobs. Remember that this is only a rough guide to potential jobs.

 Warning!

Do not be fooled into going for a job which scores fairly high overall, but which contains a few favourite factors that score really badly. For example, you really wish to work in a team (factor 8) but this job demands quite a lot of solo working (selling, for instance) – even if everything else scores really well, you could be heading off in the wrong direction if factor 8 only scores 2 or 3.

Space here for notes

2 CHECKLIST TWO - What am I good at?

The list on the following page helps you check out the particular skills and abilities that you have. Remember that you have leisure skills as well as working skills. Maybe you can use those in a job too.

Circle the letters at the end of each line for those skills that you already have and then add up the number of Ts, Is, Ps and Ds that you have. The chart on the following page shows how your score relates to the world of work. This will give you some pointers to the type of activities that best suit you. Maybe they are not the ones you are following at the present! If this is the case, then perhaps a change of direction is indicated.

As a starter on this checklist, jot down in the box below what you think are your particular skills at present – at least, those that will help you to find that good job. Then relate your notes to the particular skills listed overleaf.

I think I am pretty good at:

19

1	Being fit and physically strong	T			
2	Driving cars and trucks	T			
3	Being good with numbers		I		
4	Being good at organising			P	
5	Working from plans and diagrams				D
6	Using hand and machine tools	T			
7	Finding out how things work	T			
8	Having hand and eye co-ordination	T			
9	Sorting out data				D
10	Solving problems		I		
11	Writing good English		I		
12	Being creative		I		
13	Gathering information				D
14	Evaluating information				D
15	Leading others			P	
16	Performing intricate operations	T			
17	Mending and repairing things	T			
18	Assessing malfunctions	T			
19	Reading information and instructions				D
20	Developing good relationships			P	
21	Assessing situations and people		I		
22	Calculating and computing				D
23	Getting the best out of people			P	
24	Showing feelings and thoughts		I		
25	Motivating and praising people			P	
26	Teaching or instructing others			P	
27	Assembling things from components	T			
28	Checking lists and inventories				D
29	Designing things		I		
30	Managing money and budgets				D
31	Observing accurately				D
32	Developing other people's ideas		I		
33	Selling and persuading			P	
34	Listening to others			P	
35	Using intuition and insight		I		
36	Thinking matters through carefully		I		
37	Helping to create change			P	
38	Being sensitive to people's feeling			P	
39	Using mental arithmetic				D
40	Building and constructing	T			

Analysing Checklist Two

The letters appearing in the checklist you have just completed refer to:

T **THINGS**   **I** **IDEAS**   **P** **PEOPLE**   **D** **DATA**

The chart below identifies the main areas of work, based on these four principal factors.

If you have the highest score in Ts, then that points you in the direction of things, (practical) but if you scored high in Ps, then it is people (social or enterprising) for you. Where you have equal or nearly equal scores, the two factors will combine. For instance, if you have equal scores in Is and Ts, then your best direction is ideas and things (investigative). The chart can only give you a very rough idea based on the simple checklist you have just completed. If you are still unsure of which direction to go, then you could well benefit from advice from a careers counsellor.

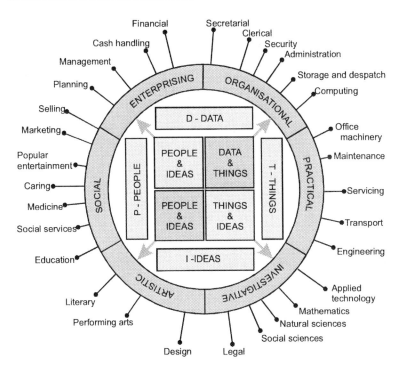

Note that it is unlikely that anyone would have an orientation that combined **people** and **things** – these two are generally mutually exclusive. Likewise a combination of **data** and **ideas** may seem to be contradictory. If you do have a score like this, you may find it slightly more difficult to find a job that includes and satisfies all your personal skills.

(Acknowledgement is given to *'Build Your Own Rainbow'* by Hopson and Scully for the inspiration for the previous exercise, published by MB2000)

Space here for notes

3   CHECKLIST THREE - Where to look?

The following are all sources of ideas for jobs. Keep them all boiling away, as the slightest hint of a good job from any of these sources is worth investigating. It is so easy to say 'don't lose hope', but a long period of job searching can be very, very depressing. Set yourself a target of so many enquiries every day and stick to it. Improve the quality of your approach as this book outlines and the waiting can be much shorter than you think.

List the names of likely sources in the boxes below and add to these as your searching becomes wider and more thorough.

1. National newspapers
dailies
weeklies

Clip out some suitable (or nearly suitable) advertisements every day. Even if the jobs are not quite for you, there is a great deal to gain from understanding what people are looking for. Never miss a day – that may be the one where your job is lurking!

---

2. Local newspapers
weeklies
freebies

Make sure that you buy your copy on publication day – get in quickly with new jobs. Scan the papers including the freebies at the first opportunity.

---

3. Trade and professional papers

These are designed to attract exactly the right people with the specialist knowledge and skills that you might have. If you cannot afford to buy your particular professional papers, then try the library or the offices of a firm in that business. Find the address of the publisher and send off for an inspection copy.

---

4. Job-finder magazines

Specialist papers in some areas designed to advertise jobs and talk generally about work and job prospects. Try and scan these papers as soon as they are published.

---

5. Local radio and television

Keep your eyes and ears open for news about new businesses and expansion plans. Even in recession, some companies are always looking for people. Find a way of videoing late night job search programmes. Note times and channels.

---

6. Signboards outside offices and factories

Never pass a likely place of potential employment without checking their vacancies board – they may change daily. A walk around a compact industrial estate calling at the various reception desks can sometimes turn up vacancies or job leads that are not advertised outside the company.

---

7. Notices in shop windows

Some smaller, local enterprises advertise (cheaply) in shop windows. Take a few moments to scan the board so that you will recognise new cards day by day.

---

8. Job Centres

An obvious source with a daily changing selection of job vacancies. It is a tragedy that so many Job Centres are closing down. In a way, it might mean that there is less unemployment – but it doesn't help you! Find the nearest – it could be well worth a trip – but do allow yourself ample time to see all that there is on offer. Ask the staff – they are there to help.

9. Clubs and pubs where people talk (not too hard, this one!)

Another ears and eyes effort, listening to conversations, letting it be known that you are hunting and that you are worth talking to (and you can have a pint at the same time!).

10. Recruitment offices

Firms that are closing down frequently offer an on-site recruitment service – well worth using.

11. Library notice boards

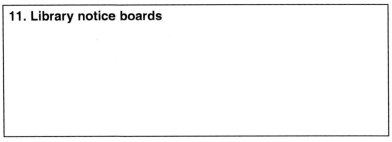

An occasional source of information about local recruitment and opportunities, especially if training is involved.

12. Conversations with neighbours and friends

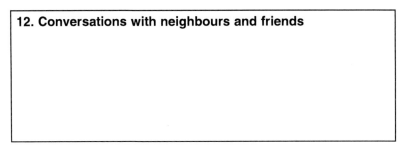

The vast majority of jobs are not advertised to the public, but made known to existing employees for passing on by word of mouth. Get in on the grapevine! This is also a sensible source of opinions about local companies that you might be targeting in your job search. Find out what people think about working for this or that firm.

13. Recruitment agencies

Make sure to have your name listed on as many agencies as possible. This is a good source of information. It needs effort on your part, especially in providing them with an excellent CV (see Checklists Sixteen to Twenty-one).

14. The internet

Technology comes to your aid!

The internet is a great source of information about job opportunities across the country. Of course, if you don't have internet access at home, your nearest library will usually have such facilities, as well as internet cafes and other access points that are springing up. There will often be people who can offer you guidance on how to get online and retrieve useful information and opportunities.

You can start by typing something like 'job vacancies UK' into a search engine (Google, Ask Jeeves and so on) and exploring what comes up, or go straight to a useful website such as any of those listed here. All offer clear instructions for finding good jobs and how to search and apply for any that are suitable.

Try looking at:

www.jobsite.co.uk
www.jobsearch.co.uk
www.education-jobs.co.uk
www.monster.co.uk
www.totaljobs.com

Take care when going down the search engine route as quite a few options shown may be American – unless you fancy pursuing your trade on the California coast ... oh, I don't know ... not so bad!

The suggestions that follow about writing off for information, doing your CV, conduct at interviews and so on, all apply equally to anything you may start on the internet. Just because you are getting all technological doesn't mean that you can forget the niceties and good practices!

It would be easy to be cynical about a checklist like this.

Or you could say that it is too obvious. You could say that:

- you have tried them all already ...
- there are thousands of other people also doing this ...
- the local situation is just impossible ...
- what's the point at my age ...
- it takes a lot of time ...
- and so on and so on ... ...

The point of the check list is to reinforce the range of possibilities that must be followed.

Never give up!

If you can find that **competitive edge** over the other people looking for jobs, you will need all these sources to give you strong leads.

Writing off to companies 'on spec' is covered later in Checklist Ten C.

Space here for notes

CHECKLIST FOUR - What's in the advertisement, anyway?

> ## WANTED NOW
> ### The best people for the very best jobs
>
> *absolutely super salary*
> **wonderful working conditions**
> BAGS OF OVERTIME
> g r e a t   l o c a t i o n
> start yesterday if you wish
> *no problems - easy work*
> blah blah blah blah blah blah blah blah
> blah blah blah blah blah blah blah blah
> blah blah blah blah
> **apply to the amazing Mr Whizzo**
> **Whizzo Works, Somewhere Near You**

Let us assume that you have found an advertisement that appeals to you. There is something about the ad that makes you think it could be a runner.

The advertisement will give you a great deal of information that you must use when you contact the company. Take care to read every line and word – ads are full of clues about exactly what the company is looking for.

The three main areas of information to look for in ads are:

A	What the company is actually looking for

B	Explanatory information about the job and the person

C	Information about the company

You must find out about all three areas of information, either from the ad or by research, *before* you tell them about you. You must be sure that you will fit their requirements and that you are in with a chance.

A What the company is actually looking for

1 Does the ad describe the job clearly?

2 Are you quite sure that you understand the description?

3 Is it one job or are there several posts?

4 Is the job title one you have ever had previously?

5 Could it describe you?

B Explanatory information about the job and the person

1 What qualifications are they seeking?

2 Have you got those qualifications?

3 What experience are they seeking?

4 Have you got that experience?

5 What education are they seeking?

6 Have you had that education?

7 Does it explain what sort of character they are seeking?

8 Is the pay quoted? Is it enough for you?

9 Is the pay stated exactly or is it 'about' so much?

10 Do you fall into the right age bracket?

11 Does it quote other benefits? Will they do for you?

12 Is the location mentioned? Will it do for you?

C Information about the company

1 Is the company name mentioned? If not, does it matter?

2 Does it explain the reason for recruiting?

3 Does it describe the company's philosophy?

4 Does it do the company credit to advertise like this?

5 Is there an equal opportunities statement?

6 How formal does the company seem to be?

7 Is the ad in a prestigious publication/a good position?

8 Does the ad suggest opportunities for training/advancement?

9 Does it describe the company's products or services?

10 Does it describe the size and scale of the company?

11 Does it explain the application processes clearly?

A good ad will contain nearly all of these points – all of which you really want to know. If the ad is rather thin on information, but the job appeals to you, then you may have to rummage around to find more details – phone them up and ask, check with friends or neighbours, visit the library.

Space here for notes

5 CHECKLIST FIVE - How to apply - the activities required

You may be required to do any of these things in any combination. All of them are carefully described and suggestions are made under the appropriate checklists. There is always a best way for these tasks and the serious job-seeker will make sure that every detail is attended to properly.

The FIVE main activities you may have to complete are:

1	Write a letter of application	(see Checklist Eleven)

2	Send for ... and complete an application form	(see Checklist Eleven) (see Checklist Fourteen)

3	Send a Curriculum Vitae	(see Checklists Sixteen to Twenty-one)

4	Send references	(see Checklist Fifteen)

1	Telephone for details	(see Checklist Eight)

Pay close attention to the the way the advertisement describes your <u>contact person</u>. The company style will tell you about the formality or informality of the firm.

- If it is in the form of **'J Alexander, Personnel Director'**, it is very systematic, rule-bound and formal.

- If it is in the form of **'Mr J Alexander'**, then it is also formal and you can expect to be called by your title and surname.

- If it is in the form of **'James Alexander'**, the company will be less formal and you can expect to be addressed by your first name.

6   CHECKLIST SIX - Analysing the advertisement

Before you even start to put pen to paper or voice to telephone, you should analyse the ad very carefully and pick out the **KEYWORDS**.

Ideally, highlight these with a marker pen or underline them carefully with a coloured biro. The following items should be highlighted.

1   **Job title**

2   **Pay rate**

3   **Main duties**

4   **Special responsibilities**

5   **Experience required**

6   **Qualifications required**

37

7   **Training required**

8   **Specific skills required**

9   **Personality required**

10   **Age limitations**

11   **Location of job**

12   **Training opportunities**

13   **Team working etc**

14   **Responsibility for others**

15   **Knowledge of the industry**

16   **Appearance and/or style**

It is important to identify all these factors as they may need to be referred to when writing letters or application forms and particularly if you are writing a special CV just for this job. (see Checklist Eighteen)

All these analyses and collections of data are vital for making the perfect letter or other approach to the company, to secure an interview. It is time well spent.

If you personally match all these 16 factors in terms of your past employments and your current hopes and expectations, then you must believe that you have a good chance of at least being interviewed. The difficulties come when you only match some of them! Or when you only match some of them half-way.

For instance, if the company is asking for five years' experience and a NVQ and you only have three years and an ONC from some time back, you have to decide whether to go ahead with the application. Quite possibly you are better-than-asked-for on other factors. This may be enough to sway the company if you write well in the first instance and then perform well at interview.

CHECKLIST SEVEN - Finding out about the company

What do you need to find out about the company before you write to them and before you go for interview? Where can you find the information you need?

A – About the company

1   How big are they locally, nationally and internationally? What turnover annually?

2   What are the main product/service lines?

3   What sort of reputation have they got? (ask around locally if you can - probably someone you know knows someone who knows!)

4   Are there any real personalities in the organisation, maybe who have been on television or in the news?

5   Do you use their products or services? Do you know someone who does? Are their products good?

6   How do they advertise their services or products? Do they produce brochures, leaflets or catalogues?

B – Where can the information be found?

1   The best source for a larger company is their <u>annual report</u>. Many such reports can be found in local libraries. Check also in the <u>Companies Register</u> or any other <u>business directories</u> such as Kompass, Jordan's, Kelly's or Sell's (ask the librarian for guidance. Check that you are looking in the most recent edition - not all are up-dated every year).

2   <u>Write separately</u> or <u>telephone</u> for a copy of their annual report and any promotional material that they produce. If you explain that you are applying for a job and wish to do your research first, you will probably be sent what you seek. File the information away in case you wish to apply to them in the future.

3   Information can be obtained from Job Centres and careers services about local firms. The local <u>newspaper</u> may carry advertisements or articles about employers in the area.

4   If the premises are not too far away, you can <u>call in</u> on some pretext and try and gauge the atmosphere and style of the place. Watch the employees leaving at the end of the day - how do they seem? Cheerful and content or cheesed off and grumpy? If you can speak to a few, what are their opinions of working there? How does it feel to be an employee? Are there any disadvantages? Be wary of mucky gossip and ill-founded prejudice!

5   If the company is quoted on the Stock Exchange, then check the shares in the <u>financial press</u>.

If all this research seems complicated and expensive on time and effort, think of this – the candidate who does not bother with it will be at a colossal disadvantage when it comes to writing or being interviewed.

After you have done the fact-finding, you will be able to ask good questions and know many of the answers that they may be looking for.

You will have a strong advantage over the others!

Space here for notes

CHECKLIST EIGHT - Telephoning to follow up an advertisement

Two responses can occur when you telephone a company about their ad; either they will merely send you their recruitment pack, or they will try to start the interview there and then. The first is no hassle – just be positive and polite when giving your name and address and be sure to say thank you at the end. You do not want a pernickety receptionist saying how rude so-and-so was when telephoning for an application form!

The second response can really catch you out if you have not yet done any homework on the organisation. Be warned! Before telephoning, at least find out something about the firm in case you are questioned.

Tips for telephoning

1   Find the <u>name of the appropriate person</u> before making the important call. It is easy to ring through beforehand and ask for the name of the personnel manager or whatever if no name is shown on the ad.

2   <u>Read all the material</u> to hand before calling - especially your highlighted advertisement. This may give you some clues as to what you might be asked.

3   Put yourself in a positive frame of mind. Never
     sound as if you are just completing a chore. Let
     them know by your enthusiasm and cheerfulness
     that this is the one job you have chosen and that
     you are just the person that they are looking for!
     Remember that this is just as much a part of your
     personal presentation package as any other. You
     must be aware that you are being assessed even
     on this small piece of contact.

4   Be prepared to answer questions. Never try to put
     off the questioning. Close your eyes and imagine
     you are in the interview room and that this is the
     real thing. Behave and respond exactly as if you
     were there.

5   Stand up! Standing up whilst speaking on the
     phone actually sounds better at the other end, as
     your posture will be good and you will be
     breathing properly. If you have several calls to
     make, be properly dressed for it! Remember the
     old BBC story about the early newsreaders having
     to wear dinner jackets? Sound advice if you wish
     to appear confident and correct on the telephone
     (well, not DJs actually, but do not do it in your
     pyjamas!).

CHECKLIST NINE - Letter writing - some general points

Let us consider for a moment the essential features of a good letter, the sort of letter that you must write to attract a favourable response. These rules apply equally to any other letter you are writing, that has any degree of formality. Think of letters from the bank, your employer, the Union, the bailiffs (maybe not) – they all show careful layout, good spelling and clear wording. Or at least, they should show these characteristics if they are to be taken seriously. The sane factors exactly must apply to your letters seeking interview or opportunity to talk about yourself.

Your letter ...

1 *must* be on <u>good, non-lined paper</u> (white is best)

2 *must* be <u>neatly written</u> (whether typed or hand-written)

3 *must* be <u>set out well</u> on the page - use space wisely and follow the current conventions of business letter writing - the example letters below are correctly laid out - try to contain the letter on just <u>one side of paper</u> if possible

4 *must* be addressed to the <u>right person</u> by name

5 *must* have <u>your address and name</u> clearly shown somewhere

6   *must* show the <u>date</u> of writing

7   *must* be in <u>good, plain English</u> with perfect grammar

8   *must* be <u>spelled correctly</u>

Note - it is frightening how arbitrary some interviewers can be! If you have serious spelling errors in your written material, this can immediately cause you to be dropped from the shortlist. The same could be said for poor grammar and bad handwriting. Never give the recruiters a chance to allow their biases and prejudices to cloud decisions about you!)

9   *must* be <u>easy to understand</u> and straight to the point

10 *must* include their <u>reference</u> if one is shown in the ad

11 *must* cover the <u>important points</u> (see Checklist Eleven)

12 *must* show you in a <u>good light</u>

13 *must* <u>conclude correctly</u> and be signed by you

14 *must* encourage the recipient to <u>ask to see you</u> in person!

It is always a good idea to have someone else check your important letters, even if you think you are pretty good at writing. Another person can often spot mistakes and unclear bits better than you can. You would not want the person who spots the silly errors to be the one you are writing to! Remember that any letter you send out in your job hunting will represent you and will form a part of your total presentation package.

Your letter must be good!

 **CHECKLIST TEN - Writing in reply to an advertisement**

There are three main approaches open to you:

| A | a letter simply asking for <u>more information</u> |

| B | a letter to <u>accompany a CV</u> if that is the company's preferred method |

| C | an actual <u>letter of application</u> where you outline your case without either an application form or a CV (this third option is covered fully in Checklist Eleven). |

Note – it is also possible to write to a company 'on spec', when they have not even advertised. The third example below shows how this can be done.

| D | Another important letter that you need to write to help your case is the <u>'yes I will attend for interview'</u> letter. This one must follow the same rules of perfect letter writing and be seen as a part of your total personal presentation package. Such a letter will create a good impression and show your commitment to their effort to recruit you. |

All the letter examples here follow the rules for good letter writing explained in Checklist Nine. Do read these rules carefully before writing letters yourself.

A. The simple 'please send more information' letter

1	**Check the name of the recipient - spell it correctly!**

2	**Be simple, grammatically correct and spell everything correctly. This is the first contact that the company will have with you, so it must be good!**

3	**After the formal start, cover only four things:** **(a) where the advertisement was seen (quote date of publication)** **(b) which job you are asking about (quote reference numbers and/or job title)** **(c) why you have a particular interest** **(d) a request to send further information and forms.**

4	**End correctly and always add your name, carefully written, after your signature.**

A simple example of such a letter is shown opposite. Note the current conventions of style and layout. These should apply even to hand-written letters. Never use lined paper, especially if torn from a notebook! (If you cannot write in straight lines on a plain sheet of paper, make a ruled grid of lines on a separate sheet. This can be clipped underneath so that you can see the lines through your letter sheet and thus guarantee that your writing is perfectly straight.)

14 Hillock Mews
Clatterton
Warwicks, CV99 9ZZ

29 Sept 2005

0999 123456
(answerphone)

Miss Julie Snetterton
Personnel Manager
Acme Servicing Company
44 Hamble Street
Coventry
Warwicks CV75 7AC

Dear Miss Snetterton

Ref: ASC/778B

Your advertisement for a Production Chargehand
(Commercial Cleaning) in today's edition of
Coventry Journal is of great interest to me. I
have completed several years experience in
commercial cleaning with Bilbow's Cleaning
Services, with responsibility for a team of
twenty operatives, using state of the art
equipment and materials.

Would you please send me the necessary application
forms and any other information about the job.
Thank you.

I look forward to hearing from you in due course.

Yours sincerely

AJobhuntr
Alec Jobhunter

Remember that if you really cannot find the name of the personnel officer and you start the letter with 'Dear Sir', then you **must** finish with 'Yours faithfully'. This is an unchangeable rule.

This simple letter covers our four requirements (see point 3 (a), (b), (c) and (d) above) and is straight to the point. You can write all the personal information on the form or send it via your CV when the time comes. It is not needed in this letter.

It must be said again (yes, it really must!) that this letter is **the first contact** that the company has with you, so it must be very good. It must encourage further contact from them, not make them say, 'This person must be joking'.

B. The 'Here is my CV' letter

Generally the advertisement will have said something like 'write in the first instance, enclosing a CV'. They may also ask for current earnings.

The letter you send must not duplicate the information in the CV (which, of course, must be totally up-to-date), except to emphasise one or two important points from the advertisement, if this seems sensible.

14 Hillock Mews
Clatterton
Warwicks, CV99 9ZZ

14 October 2005

0999 123456
(answerphone)

Miss Julie Snetterton
Acme Servicing Company 👈 (note that the address should be in full
Coventry   as in the previous example letter)

Dear Miss Snetterton

Ref: ASC/PC22

Your advertisement in today's Coventry Journal is
of great interest to me and I would like to
apply for the post of Production Controller.
    The enclosed Curriculum Vitae shows that I
have several years' experience in an organisation
similar to yours, but in a more junior position,
although with an overall greater budgetary
responsibility. I recently passed with Honours
the Advanced Production Controller Diploma at
Coventry College and was awarded the Johnson
Poppleton Prize. The project examined the
advanced use of the Schlam-Flinger process for
short run production, which I know is a current
interest of your company.
    I feel sure that my experience and training
as outlined in the CV fit me very well for the
post you outline and I would be pleased to
attend your offices for interview. I look forward
to hearing from you in due course.

Yours sincerely

Mary Jobhunter
Mary Jobhunter

Note the inclusion of a telephone number on the letterhead and the mention of an answerphone facility. Simple answering machines are very cheap these days and could be a sensible investment to guarantee your receiving offers of interview.

C. The 'on spec' letter (no advertisement yet)

If there is an organisation that you wish to contact, just to tell them about yourself and to see if they have any vacancies, you need to send a very clear letter. It must introduce you and the reason for writing. You should enclose a good general CV.

A simple approach that is straight to the point is appropriate. The letter must be like those brochures that plonk onto your doormat that you do look at – it must attract immediately. Try and pick out a feature of your past work that might appeal to the company, something that you did very well that they might need too.

One effective way of homing straight in to the personnel manager is to find his or her name, and address the letter direct. (Do make sure you spell the name correctly.)

The example letter shown opposite is one such 'this is me – please employ me' type of letter.

14 Hillock Mews etc

14 October 2005

Miss Julie Snetterton   (note that all addresses should

be in full)

Dear Miss Snetterton

May I take a moment of your time to introduce
myself. At present I am seeking to expand my
experience in the servicing industry and I feel
that I could offer Acme Servicing Company a
wealth of experience and a comprehensive clutch
of skills.

The enclosed CV covers the detail of my
working life so far. The entry against my work
at Plonker's Servicing Ltd shows the range of
responsibilities that I enjoyed and the extent of
my supervisory control, with thirty-five staff.

The budget I managed was in excess of half a
million pounds and I was privileged to represent
Plonkers at the Annual Servicing Exhibition at
the NEC in 1997.

I would be very pleased to know of any
vacancies that you may have at present or in the
near future for senior supervisory staff. I
understand that you are expanding your operations
to the Home Counties shortly - I can be very
mobile and would relish a new area.

It is hoped that the information in this
letter and the CV will encourage you to see me
to discuss the possibility of my joining your
organisation. I look forward to hearing from you
in due course.

Yours sincerely

Mary Jobhunter

Mary Jobhunter

Space here for notes

11 CHECKLIST ELEVEN - Applying for a job by letter

You may be asked to write just a **letter of application** without adding a CV or any other material. Such a request may be to help the company do some **initial sifting** of applicants. This means that you do not have to write your entire life history in the letter – wait for the application form to arrive and use that.

- Once they have received all the letters, the company will then send out application forms to the **best of the bunch.**

- <u>You</u> want to be in that bunch so your letter must be **GOOD!**

The factors in Checklist Nine (Good letter writing) are not too difficult until it comes to item 11, 'must cover the important points'. What are the important points to include in a letter of application that will help you be put on the best-of-bunch list?

Factors to include

1 what this letter is about (e.g. applying for job no. X)

2 why you would be suited to the job

3 why the job would be suited to you

4 special features about you that will be of particular interest to the company

5 a statement about your determination to put your very best efforts into the company's activities

6 a request to be given the chance to talk the matter.

A simplified example of such a letter is shown below. It conforms with all the ideas shown in Checklist Nine and it also includes the six items above as shown by the numbers (1) to (6) at the side of the text. Do not for heaven's sake put these numbers on your letter! They are for your guidance only. The text is also just for guidance, although there are phrases and ideas that you could well use in your own letters. Do try to be original and be sure to make the letter relevant to the post being applied for.

```
(Their name and address)      (Your address and
                                          telephone)
(Date)
              ☞ (usual headings and addresses, of course!) ☝

Dear ... (correct name or 'Sir')


Reference no. ... (as appropriate, from the advertisement)


I saw with great interest your advertisement in
last night's edition of the ... and I would like
to apply for the post of ... (add in appropriate words)

My recent four years' employment with Messrs ...
has given me a great deal of relevant experience
in the field that you describe in the
advertisement. I am experienced in ..., familiar
with ..., have used extensively ... After only
five months there, I was promoted to Foreman in
their ... Department and the added responsibility
has done much for my confidence and my abilities
to deal effectively with a mixed, technical
workforce. I controlled a budget of ...,
completed a major project on ... (add in appropriate words)


The job you describe would seem to be a very
sensible and logical step in my chosen career
```

development. The challenge of working with a
company like yours with its fine national
reputation for excellence will help me to achieve
my goals.

At present I am nearing the end of a three-year
part-time course in ... and I am confident of
passing. I understand that you are keen to employ
fully qualified personnel and this course has
given me a great insight into our industry. It
has also given me a broad understanding of the
current technology and likely future
developments.

I can assure you that I will put my best efforts
into helping your company to continue its growth
and prosperity.

I hope that this letter will encourage you to
ask for further information about me and that we
can eventually meet for an interview.

Yours ... ('sincerely' or 'faithfully' according to your opening greeting)

    (Signature)

(Your name, carefully written)

Space here for notes

 **CHECKLIST TWELVE - What might the company send you?**

You are very likely to receive any or all of these items.

1 | an <u>application form</u> to be filled in and returned

2 | a <u>Job Description</u> and <u>Person Specification</u>
(many organisations combine these two documents into one, sometimes called a Job Specification - see the box overleaf)

3 | <u>information</u> about the company

4 | details of <u>what to do next</u>, such as closing dates for applications and the address to which to send the appropriate papers

The very first thing to do is read them all very carefully. There will be a number of clues about the sort of person they are looking for, about the way they expect you to respond and about the company itself. If an application form is sent, spend a few pennies on a photocopy. Never write straight away onto a new form without testing out the spaces and layout first. (see Checklist Fourteen)

Look for all the points mentioned in Checklists Four and Six. You can also highlight any new information in the details you have been sent about the company. It is all evidence to help you make a good attempt at the application form or the appropriate version of your CV.

Be sure that you note any closing dates for applications – it would be terrible if you missed the date after taking all the trouble to get the information.

Filling in the application form, is covered in Checklists Thirteen and Fourteen.

Additional information

Job description and person specification

A **Job Description** is a written document that outlines the tasks and duties to be performed by a particular job-holder. It says what has to be done, where the responsibility lies, what accountability there is and details about the physical, social and financial conditions that apply. **It describes the JOB.**

A **Person Specification** is a written document that outlines the characteristics and personal abilities and skills of the ideal job holder. **It describes the JOB-HOLDER.**

Many companies put bits of both documents into one single **Job Specification.**

 **CHECKLIST THIRTEEN - Application forms**

Let us agree that there should be a national standard for application forms – every company seems to have its own version. Perhaps this should be built into the next all-party government election manifestos!

When you have completed an application form, the information you have written rarely seems to fit the next one you try. This can be really irritating – but you are stuck with it.

(See also Checklist Twenty-six for a simple but effective method for recording important information.)

1	**Make a copy of each form you intend to send back, before you write anything on it. You can use this photocopy for practice at fitting your information into the spaces provided.** **Note:** An alternative way is to buy some cheap tracing paper and clip that over the form to practice space filling.

2	**Unless you are a brilliant typist and can fit typewriting into small boxes, write by hand. Often companies ask for hand-written forms.** **Note:** It can be unwise to get someone else to do it for you, even if your hand-writing is fairly bad. You may be caught out if asked to write anything else at the interview, or even later on, at work.

3

When you have filled in a very comprehensive form, with all your work history and a personal statement, make a copy of it before you send it off. This can be very useful as a source of reference for other forms. It is very irritating to have to think through all the details again and again.

Note: An alternative to this approach is to make for yourself the 'absolute personal data file' - with absolutely everything in it, each job in all its glory and every bit of personal detail. Keep this to one side and use it as your master reference, adding bits as you think of them (see Checklist Twenty-six).

4

Some firms use just one application form for all their recruiting, so do not be surprised if the boxes for some items are enormous! This may be to accommodate the experience or qualifications of older and more highly trained personnel. There is no rule about having to completely fill up every box!

Note: It is also generally true that companies are content if you write extra information on a separate sheet if there really is insufficient room on the form - but don't overdo it. The recruiter does not want to disappear behind ever-increasing mountains of papers from potential employees!

14 CHECKLIST FOURTEEN - Filling in an application form

The system of recording personal information as described in Checklist Twenty-six is for your use as a permanent reference. You should take some time to complete the cards, working over several days if necessary. Refine the points you write down and add more as time goes by. This can then be your starting point for any application form that comes your way. You won't have to rummage in your mind for the facts of your working life, they will all be spread out in detail on the cards. You can then copy out the appropriate bits quite quickly.

Having a central file of all the important parts of your personal information together with notes about best practice in job-hunting makes sense. That is why we recommended that you complete all the lists and example documents in the book. When you have your card file and your CV as well, then you have the complete kit!

The standard type of application form contains spaces for answers to a range of questions. We shall look at each one in turn ...

1. Names

Make it clear which are your first names and which is the family or surname.

2. Address

Make it clear which is the address where information should be sent, especially if you are living away from home.

3. Telephone number

If you are in employment and it would be dangerous or embarrassing to take calls at work, then make this quite clear too.

4. Age and status

Always be completely honest about these. The information may be used for taxation and national insurance purposes. You may also be asked to quote your National Insurance Number (the one that looks like AA 12 34 56 D).

As with most aspects of this job-search business, once you start distorting the truth or stretching or omitting facts, you will be hard pressed to remember what you said and are very likely to get caught out. Then all your credibility is shot and you can say goodbye to what might have been a great opportunity.

5. Employment history

The space for this information will vary tremendously from form to form. There are five sensible recommendations about filling in this section:

(a) **Start with the current or most recent job and work backwards**. The Personnel Officer will be more interested in what you have been doing recently than in activities twenty years ago. Some forms have a separate, larger box for your present (or most recent) employment.

(b) **Write in detail about the most recent jobs** (or an earlier job that is very relevant to the job being applied for)

(c) Always **highlight the things that you have done** which have a direct bearing on the job being applied for. The papers from the company will give you many clues about what they are looking for in terms of experience and progress. Relate your own working history with these requirements in mind. Always be factual and do not claim to have done things that you have not done. Do not claim areas of responsibility that you did not have. Do not use phrases like 'considerable involvement' when you only attended one ten-minute meeting once a month!

(d) If you are asked to give details of salary, enter your **leaving salary**. Do not exaggerate – you may talk yourself out of a good job.

(e) Where you are asked **reasons for leaving**, be careful in your choice of words. Redundancy and the business folding are likely to excite sympathy. Getting the sack or 'I couldn't get on with the boss' are likely to excite curiosity and doubt. Never apportion blame to others, talk about being overworked or claim that it was for 'personal reasons' – these will also raise doubts in the interviewer's mind. Whatever you write, it must not look as if you are unreliable, a troublemaker or just plain lazy.

6. Qualifications and training

These areas are often very important in proving that you are exactly the person the company is looking for. You need to study the advertisement or the papers that the company has sent to you. Then decide what you need to emphasise and what you can keep quiet about.

(a) Professional qualifications

Professional qualifications are very important in some occupations where you will be expected to have passed examinations in order to work at all. In other occupations, they hardly matter, except to say what level of education you reached at some time. Whatever the situation, never lie about qualifications or invent some you have not got. The employer may check up. Finding lies and inventions can put everything else you have said into jeopardy.

(b) Educational qualifications

List your educational qualifications with the best (or the most appropriate for the job) at the top and work backwards to exams passed at school. It is not generally necessary to list the subjects covered in a degree course unless they are relevant to the job. Similarly it is not necessary to list grades in GCEs and GCSEs, merely list the passes.

(c) Schooling

There may be a request to include schooling. If this was a long time ago, just mention the name of the school. Certainly no-one need refer back to anything before secondary education.

(d) Examinations

If you studied for some examinations but did not pass, you can include it if the study itself would be relevant to the job. You may have to explain the failure during your interview, but at least the company will know that you were thought to be capable of studying to that level.

(e) Industrial or commercial training

The same considerations apply to industrial or commercial training received during your working life. Mention courses completed if they seem appropriate to the job, or if you wish to show that you have tried to better yourself during your career. The name of the course, the year and the supplier or location will usually suffice. People in your business will recognise significant courses.

7. Personal statements

This is often the most difficult part of the form to complete, the section headed 'In a few words, tell us about yourself' or 'Is there anything else you wish to add about yourself that is not covered elsewhere?' The clue is 'not covered elsewhere' – do not be duped into writing bits again and repeating information that you have already given. One excellent way to complete this section is to use material from your CV, especially the profile (see Checklist Nineteen), and adapt it as appropriate to the job.

The reason many companies employ this type of space on a form is to make you exercise your mind, make you think. They want to know if you can be creative, write effectively and be persuasive. Use it to add any relevant points that cannot be put in anywhere else. Use it to create a powerful summary of your career to date and your ideal candidature for the job in question. You do not have to fill the space. Once you have composed a really good personal statement, keep a copy and use it as a basis for others. Change a word here, a word there, and you can flex the statement to most situations.

Remember that your personal statement is often a major source of questions from the interviewer, so make sure that what you write is factual – also ...

- do not exaggerate your own abilities
- do not claim to have done things you have not done
- never write too boastfully or pompously
- sing your own praises by all means – this is the first real picture of yourself
- you are sending to the company so it has to be good
- do not go over the top – you will be found out!

The personal statement is really quite difficult to do well - and it should be re-written for each application, to match what they are looking for, if possible. It is one of the bits of the application process that benefits from being checked over by a friend who knows you well, but who isn't afraid to offer critical comments.

A cautionary story

Many, many years ago, the author applied within his own company for a senior post in Human Resource Management which at that time was called Manpower Planning. During the interview, which was in front of several very senior people he already knew from the organisation, the question was raised about his participation in the processes of manpower planning, as he had written on the application form that he had *'substantial involvement in several aspects of manpower planning'*. Under increasingly hostile questioning, he had to admit that he had attended a couple of local meetings of the Manpower Society and had read a few magazine articles. Oops! That was about it. The man leading the interview looked across and said, smiling, *'Okay, James, shall we stop the interview here?'* Of course, no promotion and quite a bit of loss of face. Take heed! Don't try and spoof!

8. Interests and hobbies

There is doubt in some people's minds about the relevance of a person's leisure interests to his or her job. However, the interviewer may wish to assess whether your hobbies and leisure interests are merely 'an interest in' meaning that you like to watch it on television or 'I participate in' meaning that you have skills and play, compete or actively pursue a pastime.

There may be suspicion about a radio engineer whose only hobby is mending radios (very narrow interests), but acceptance of a desk-worker who plays local team football to compensate for a sedentary job (good balance of activities). Include hobbies and leisure interests if they give a broader picture of you as a person, but do not write long essays about your skills or interests!

9. Health and Medical History

Always be truthful about your medical history. If you have had serious illness or injury but are now fully recovered, say so. Mention any disability. Be truthful also about days off work – remember that these facts can be checked.

10. Referees

(this is covered by Checklist Fifteen)

11. Miscellaneous extras

Because there is no standardisation of application forms, you may come across a variety of extra boxes and questions. Always try to be accurate and honest in filling in details about yourself. The company probably has a good reason for asking these questions – you do not want to spoil your chances by putting scrappy answers down.

Some of the areas covered by these extra questions are:

(a) periods of notice and possible start dates

(b) names of people you know who already work there

(c) information about any convictions and dates (if this applies to you, make sure that you understand the provisions of the Rehabilitation of Offenders Act 1974 and the concept of 'spent conviction')

(d) where you found the advertisement or information about the job

(e) professional association or trade union memberships

(f) questions about special skills and areas of knowledge that might be needed for the job or the company, such as proficiency in languages, knowledge of ISO9000 etc, or employment law, ability to drive or possession of a first aid certificate.

Space here for notes

15 CHECKLIST FIFTEEN - Referees and references

There are very few organisations that do not ask for references. This is strange as no one is likely to give the name of a referee who will write terrible things or say 'don't touch him with a barge pole'! However, often the job will be offered 'subject to satisfactory references' and this usually includes the present or immediate past employer. If you left the last job under a cloud or after a disastrous row with the boss, then you have to take a chance on the reference not being too bad.

Choosing referees is important, no matter what you think of the value of their references.

| 1 | Choose at least **one person who can speak well about your working life**. This is usually your present (or last) boss, but could be someone from another fairly recent employment. You can also name a senior person from your work who is (was) not your direct line manager, but who has good experience of your working patterns and abilities. |

| 2 | Choose at least **one person who can speak well about you in connection with your private life** - a character reference. This can be an individual of some local importance, a colleague from your leisure activities or a professional person you have dealt with. Do not use relatives. |

| 3 | Always **ask your referees** if they would be willing to give you references. If you are likely to try for quite a number of jobs, the task of being a referee can be arduous, so you can help by promising to copy a standard reference that can be used for several jobs, with only a simple change of addresses and recipients' names. |

4 A **reference** is usually asked for by potential employers. A **testimonial** is a general letter from a past employer which usually starts with the words, 'to whom it may concern'. Testimonials may be of use on occasions, but do not use any that are really old. They rarely say anything bad and merely prove that you worked for the writer at some time. If your last employer gave you a really glowing testimonial that does show you in a very good light, then that can be used effectively.

5 When writing details of your referees, put their **correct titles** in and say what the **relationship** between you is.

List here some people you might be able to use as references

(a) Work-related references

(a) Character-related references

16 CHECKLIST SIXTEEN - What is important about having a quality CV?

Without a shadow of doubt, a well composed and beautifully produced **Curriculum Vitae** is your best marketing aid. We call it a 'marketing aid' because it is the brochure about you, the pamphlet or leaflet that describes **this fantastic product that you are offering – YOURSELF!**

There are several vital points to be made before we start to build your own CV.

1 # It has to be GOOD!

2 It has to attract the <u>attention</u> of the recruiter right at the start.

3 It must be <u>neat</u>, perfectly presented and (preferably) an <u>original</u>.

4 It must be designed to <u>market</u> you

5 You need a <u>standard</u> 'marketing aid' for general use - one which you could send out at a moment's notice

6 You also need to be able to construct one for a <u>special purpose</u>, when a really super job looms on the horizon and you need special effort

TAKE IT FROM THE HORSE'S MOUTH	Point 1 in the list on the previous page is written in huge letters for a good reason - your CV must be the very best that you can do. It is such an important document in the business of selling **YOU**. It has to be good. Professional recruiters are very critical about the material sent in by prospective employees - especially about CVs and application forms. Very often it can be seen that very little care has been taken in producing the material, with stupid mistakes, spelling errors, lack of grammar and general untidiness and sloppiness. *One recruiter, faced with some 120 applications for a particular job, went through the entire pile in about twenty minutes, making a swift assessment of each and discarding individual applications just on the basis of an instant judgement about their immediate appearance and appeal as a written document. Undoubtedly, some good candidates lost out on this rather arbitrary approach, but he said that if the papers did not look good there and then, he would not consider the applicant.*

17 CHECKLIST SEVENTEEN - How do you make your CV stand out from the rest?

YOUR CV
HAS GOT TO STAND OUT
FROM THE REST!

ĦЄRЄ IS CĦЄ CV уою ĦΛVЄ
BЄЄN WΛITING FOR
Pow! I'm the one your company needs!
Jennifer Wonder-Woman
Pie-in-the-Sky Cottage
Everyone knows where that is

Experience - I have beeneverywhere, done everything, worked for millionnaires, super-stars and captains of industry. I am an absolute goddess, adored by all and feted and fancied from Timbuktu to Turin, Tokyo to Texas. Your outfit needs me, now!

What more do you need - just send me the start date and we will be partners for evermore - so there!

Think for a moment about the mass of leaflets and brochures of all sizes, shapes and colours that plop onto your doormat every week – they fall out of magazines, they are posted by hopeful salesmen, they are sent round by charities and social groups. What is **different** about the one leaflet that you actually read? Is it the style, the layout, the picture on the front, the fact that it is about a topic that interests you?

Something made it stand out from the rest. Your CV has got to do that and make the recipient say, 'Wow! This one I must read!'

Remember the story 'from the horse's mouth' that was highlighted a couple of pages back? The recruiter only looked at the applications (including CVs) that really stood out from the mass of material that he received that day. The ones he chose to pursue further were the ones that stood out from the rest. **Yours has got to be one of those!**

Three critical factors about good CVs

1

So, do you write it in purple ink? Do you write it on fluorescent yellow paper? Do you paste on a photograph? Do you have an embossed gold border? No doubt all these have been tried. The answer is the one thing that all those odd-ball ideas also cover - presentation.

The first factor is presentation

You make a decision about the doormat leaflet in an instant - pick it up, decide what you think about it, throw it away or read it. It takes only seconds. Once you have decided to look at it more closely, you read the key words that stand out from the rest. Then another decision - do you read any more? If those first words were exciting, for whatever reason, you read on to the end.

2

Let us apply the same psychology to your CV and the person you are sending it to. Probably it is one among dozens that the recruiter has received. So, she picks it up, sees that it is perfectly laid out with neat, consistent writing and obvious care. So far so good. Then he or she will read the key words.

The second factor is the key words

The key words need to be put together with great care - they form the equivalent to the picture or photograph in the holiday brochure.

3

The follow-on material must also be good, but it will tend to confirm what the reader found in the key words section. But this will only apply if the CV is relevant to the job that the recruiter is trying to fill.

The third factor is relevance

The CV must be relevant and this means that you probably need to re-write your CV for each major application. However, a standard, basic, all-encompassing CV will do for many occasions. Never try to cook your own books. Any blurring of the truth or exaggerated or false claims will be found out - to your great loss!

Back to the brochure concept for a moment – when a leaflet falls onto your mat or out of your weekend paper, you probably check it out along the following lines.

TRAVEL IN COMFORT
with XYZ airline

This is the way to travel - take a private plane to wherever you wish to go - just like having a car and chauffeur in the sky

sdapojsd aerp ncpe ofaph pi pdf jjv nav mbae eg a maqakg lgp tb kwnnx cn kfds basjdpjr pas fpas fm pclae po dlpo hnmldsvpk skjdj nc ajcpadj er sdapojsd aerp ncpe ofaph pi pdf jjv nav mbae eg a maqakg lgp tb kwnnx cn kfds basjdpjr pas fpas fm pclae po dlpo hnmldsvpk skjdj nc psd okg ajcpadj er psd okg

You will look at the image first **(men + plane)** – this catches your attention best. If you like it, then you read the main caption **(Travel in Comfort)**. If that still holds your attention, then you look at the sub-headings **(This is the way to travel …)** and finally, if you are still interested, you read the small print.

Your CV must be constructed in a similar fashion – there must be something which instantly grabs the recruiter's attention, maybe a simple yet effective word picture of yourself.
(see Checklist Nineteen for details of how to do this)

Photographs?

Some people attach a photograph of themselves to the CV. Think very carefully about this one. If appearance is critical for the job (model, salesperson, receptionist, interviewer) then it might help if you fit the probable criteria. If you are a scruffy, spotty individual, then rely on your *words* to get you in and then show the interviewers what a wonderful and talented person you really are underneath the rough exterior!

18 CHECKLIST EIGHTEEN - The parts of a perfect CV

The following sections describe the various elements of a perfect CV, which should contain details about four areas of your background and working experience.

a	**your personal details**
b	**information about your education and qualifications**
c	**information about your career history**
d	**leisure interests and other involvements**

 The data collection system described in Checklist Twenty-six shows you how to compile the data needed for your CV.

Your CV should have the following parts, which we will look at in turn over the next few pages.

1 Name
2 Address
3 Personal details (optional)
4 Personal Profile (covered in detail in Checklist Nineteen)
5 Employment History
6 Education and Training
7 Leisure Interests
8 Contact names or Referees (optional)

Name

Start with your name in bold lettering – just first name(s) and surname, no title unless you have a courtesy title (Dame, Sir, Lady, Lord etc). Any title indicating gender or status (Mr, Mrs, Miss, Ms, Dr, Rev etc) can be implied later in the personal details.

Many people start their CVs by writing **'Curriculum Vitae'** in bold letters across the top of the first sheet. This is not absolutely necessary as anyone reading the document will know what it is.

Address

Put your address next with the post code and telephone number (remember to include the area code and postcode).

Personal details (optional)

A favourite error is then to put masses of personal information that really is not needed, such as age, date of birth, size and composition of family, marital status, birthmarks, inside leg measurement and name of cat!

The inclusion of age at all is an arguable point. It rather depends on your age at the time of writing and the way it coincides or does not coincide with the requirements in the advertisement! Your career history and details of your education will give good clues about your age. If the recruiter needs to know the ages of applicants and yours is not shown, you may be at a disadvantage if he or she has to calculate it. It is a difficult decision. Obviously, if you are appointed, your age will be important for calculating salary and pension rates and if you get as far as an interview, you will be asked. You must choose whether to be bold or slightly coy about your age!

In spite of the fact that it is unlawful to discriminate on grounds of marital status and just plain unfair to make employment decisions on the number of children, being divorced or having dependent dotty grannies, it is still done by some recruiters. Avoid the risk by leaving out such personal minutiae.

There is quite a large raft of legislation that concerns discrimination of one sort or another and most recruiters are very clear in their minds about the law. However, you should not be questioned on 'discriminatory' topics.

Personal profile

Remember the doormat brochure you actually read – the one with the appealing picture and few words? The next item after name and address (which could actually be put at the bottom for dramatic effect) is the 'key words' bit – the personal profile.

 This is the most important part of your CV, the element of the CV that grabs attention.

It is dealt with separately and in detail in Checklist Nineteen.

Employment history

This is the second most important part of your CV. It is dealt with separately and in detail in Checklist Twenty.

Education and training

Education and training must be covered in an appropriate fashion for the type and nature of the job application. You must examine the advertisement and other material from the company very carefully to see exactly what they are looking for. Then match your statements about your education and training as closely as possible. If you cannot quite come up to the requirements, state your actual educational achievements in as favourable a light as you can. Highlight the fact that you are nearly there and that you are willing to take further training if needed. Many people, the writer included, have been offered posts where an apparently vital qualification was missing, but where other characteristics and abilities amply made up for the absence.

Note – If you are 'of mature years', then the inclusion of '0' and 'A' levels and GCSEs may be rather irrelevant on a CV. Try to estimate what level of information the employer will be looking for – if you have a degree, then assumptions can be made about your schooling; if you have the relevant professional memberships, assumptions can be made about your career status; if you only have one GCSE, then it is best left out rather than be put in to stand shivering on its own! Remember that the interviewer will be looking for a structural engineer with experience, not someone who passed RSA Metalwork twenty-five years ago!

(a) Education

All the following points are valid, when assembling your education details.

- Do *not* list all the schools you have attended since the age of four or five.

- Only name schools where you spent a substantial time, or where you finished your basic education – there is no need to add the schools' addresses.

- Only name schools at the secondary and tertiary levels.

- It is often sufficient to list only your successful examinations, without saying where you achieved them.

- Unless a specific subject is mentioned in the company's materials, a simple list of passes will generally be sufficient without quoting all the separate subjects that were studied to make up the qualification.

- It may be sensible to list courses followed that did not result in passes if it gives an indication to the employer of the level you worked at, even if you eventually failed.

- More and more employers will be seeking people with NVQs (National Vocational Qualifications), so be sure to list these carefully. As these are relatively recent qualifications, older ONC, HNC, City and Guilds and other qualifications are still very important, to prove your skills and competence.

- Always state the grade of a degree and quote designatory letters of professional institutes rather than just saying 'member of'.

- For simplicity's sake, list schools/colleges separately from qualifications – see the following examples.

Qualifications	Education
1987 Post-graduate Dip Ed	1983-7 Leeds Polytechnic
1986 BSc 1/2 Food Science	
1983 'A' Levels in Chemistry, Physics,	1976-83 Corveston School
Mathematics and English	Somerset
1981 'O' Levels in English, Maths, French,	
Geography and Economics	

Qualifications	Education
1983 Cert in Social Service	1981-3 Middlewich College
	(part-time)
1963 'O' Level in English and Art	1958-63 Various Army
	schools in Europe and Asia

(b) Training

- If you have passed recognised training courses, these can be listed.

- Be clear about the nature of the course, when you did it and where.

- Do not list all the little in-company courses that you may have done – concentrate on the ones where the potential employer will be impressed, or where that training is essential for the job.

- The information must be precise and understandable to people who may not be very familiar with the courses you mention – see the following example.

Specialist Training

1988	Swindon College - Use of Abrasive Wheels
1986	St John Ambulance - Advanced First Aid
1984-5	Megatrim Ltd - Full In-house Supervisory Management Programme

---

Leisure interests

Leisure interests are noted in the final section of the CV. These need to be short entries covering your main interests – try to limit the list to six at most. Single word entries are not helpful – 'football' can mean anything from being the star player in a non-league side to watching the results on television for the pools! 'Local league football player' or 'Avid Rovers supporter' are more meaningful.

Do not list interests or pastimes that you do not actually follow. You can fall foul of the interviewer if you try to spoof your way. Interviewers will be looking for evidence of interests that show whether you are a thinker or a doer, a team person or a loner, or whether you favour leisure pursuits that are physical, intellectual, social, solitary, sedentary or active. Ideally, you should have a good mix of interests. What would you think of a person who worked all day in a factory making alarm clocks and whose one and only hobby was repairing alarm clocks? Rather limited?

You may also list such attributes as holding a full driving licence or your skills with language(s).

Referees and references (optional)

This topic has been covered in Checklist Fifteen.

19 | CHECKLIST NINETEEN - The personal profile in the CV

This critically important element of your CV needs very careful composition and must be the **personal pen-portrait** that will promote the idea of you as the ideal employee for this particular job.

Your PERSONAL PROFILE should have three parts:

a	**a description of you as a professional**
b	**the main areas of expertise that you have developed being that sort of professional**
c	**the specific skills you have needed to be the success that you are**

These should be short but carefully composed paragraphs. They must be factual and relevant to the job for which you are applying. They should be written in the first person and must be grammatically perfect. This profile will be the first words the recruiter reads about you, so they must be good enough to get you onto that best-of-bunch list we mentioned some time back. From a visual point of view, it is effective to enclose these statements in a box frame.

Overleaf is an example of a profile (guess who wrote this one!)

See the notes that follow.

PERSONAL PROFILE

I am an experienced manager, human resources manager, business consultant, trainer and author, having developed my career in several industries. I am now using that wealth of experience in a very broad spectrum of publishing, consultancy and human resource development.

Within these roles I have developed expertise in management and supervisory techniques, personnel procedures and industrial relations, human resource management and training and teaching practice. A particular interest is researching and writing about management practice and improving personal performance at all levels in organisations. I am a published author in these areas.

My success in these areas has required a wide range of skills including analytical problem solving and lateral thinking, counselling and tutoring, communication, creative and innovative writing and speaking.

Notes on the format of the Personal Profile

(a) Paragraph one identifies **the range of activities and occupations** held in the past and the present (in only two short sentences). *These listed occupations must be chosen to coincide with the job in question.* If you have had other occupations, mention them later by all means but they will not attract like the ones that are relevant.

(b) Paragraph two goes beyond job titles and states sharply **what areas of expertise exist** *(again, these must be chosen with relevance to the job)*. Note the 'particular interest', carefully shown up as very relevant to the job.

(c) Paragraph three is even more focused. It identifies **specific skills** – and also claims **'success'**.

Your 'brochure' must point out, right at the start, the essential characteristics of the person you are trying to 'sell'.

Make them want to buy!

Here is another example from a person with only one real area of working experience.

PERSONAL PROFILE

I am a competent, experienced telephone sales executive, with several years' acknowledged and fruitful work for a range of organisations whose success depends on their excellent interactions and dealings with the public. In addition, I have a sound working knowledge of administrative and office control systems.

My success in these areas has been due to a delight in meeting with and talking to members of the public and associated co-professionals, good training and advice from colleagues and managers, and opportunities to develop new skills and take on wider responsibilities.

I would consider my major assets to be enthusiasm for life, an ability to motivate others, a cheerful and sociable outlook, a thorough grasp of the principles of good client care and a courteous and efficient telephone manner.

It is important to avoid using very emotive words that would only be used when describing a national figure. Such words are charismatic, genius, born leader, exciting, superlative. Avoid also trendy clichés that can upset the recruiter, such as 'at the sharp end', 'at the cutting edge', 'on the back burner'.

This box is the zappy, sharp word-picture that makes 'em want you.

Space here for notes

20 CHECKLIST TWENTY - Employment history

The part of the CV which covers your employment history has to be crisp and clear. Let us first look at a favoured style of presentation and then we can consider what has to go into each section.

Jan 2000 - Mar 2004	**Sales Supervisor, Children's Clothes**
	Hansel and Gretel Stores, South Wigton

Responsible for the supervision and control of six sales assistants, for display, general tidiness and supervision of till operations. Shared responsibility for stocktaking and ordering. Represented the children's clothes sales team at departmental meetings.

This style is very simple to follow and takes the reader's eyes straight to the four essential elements of each job outline.

1 **The dates** - these should be shown clearly at the start of each entry. If you wish to present a complete picture, then the month should be shown too (choose a simple three-letter abbreviation). Note that smallish gaps in your employment history can be disguised by using year dates only, but a keen interviewer will notice this and ask you to explain!

2 **The job title** - this needs to be underlined as the title is often more relevant than the company worked for, when scanning down a list of jobs.

3 **The company name** - this is important, but need not include the full address. If enquiries need to be made, the interviewer will ask for the details.

89

4	**A synopsis of work undertaken** - this should include major responsibilities and highlighted aspects that are relevant to the job being applied for. Of course, jobs you did many years ago are probably not relevant nowadays, so keep the entry small. The job descriptions should become more explanatory and illustrative the more recent they are, particularly if the job you are seeking is a logical continuation from your present or last job.

Two styles are popular

(a) the style used in the example above, with crisp statements of the 'been there, done that' variety. The statements are not strictly complete sentences, but they do avoid repeating phrases such as 'I was responsible for … ' or 'I did …'

(b) a more correct style grammatically, using 'I' more and putting the whole scene in the first person. The above example would therefore read:

'I was responsible for the supervision and control of six sales assistants, for display, general tidiness and supervision of till operations. I shared responsibility for stocktaking and ordering and I represented the children's clothes sales team at departmental meetings.'

Whichever approach you choose, you must compile the information carefully. Refer to your master file of job details and select those aspects of the job that will show how suitable you are for the job being applied for.

Remember that you need to flex the wording to reflect the requirements of the advertiser if you are making a job-specific CV. Emphasise the skills that they are seeking and the areas of knowledge that they have specified.

21 | CHECKLIST TWENTY-ONE - Putting the CV together

Before actually writing the draft of your CV, you will have to assemble all the necessary information. The best way to do this is to start a card file with all the separate bits of information listed on the appropriate card. You would have cards for each job you have had, which would include data about title, company, dates, duties, wages, promotions, courses, reasons for leaving; cards for education and qualifications; lists of hobbies; the information you plan to put into the profile and so on.

A suggested system using cards is explained fully in Checklist Twenty-six. Keep adding data as it occurs to you to make up a complete portrait of your working life. Then you can pick out the bits you need for each application or CV.

The following points are all vital in producing a sensible, pleasing, effective and interview-catching CV.

1	Try very hard to confine your CV to two sides of A4 paper (the size of these two pages of this book opened flat) at the most.
2	Always produce your CV on top quality paper (white for preference, although pale shades of blue or grey look distinguished, provided your accompanying letters are on the same sort of paper).
3	Always have your CV typed or computer produced. Try to find a system that will allow you to produce covering letters by the same process. If you do not type or have access to a computer, find a kind friend who will do it for you for a modest payment. The net effect of a carefully typed CV is so much greater than a hand-written one, even if you have perfect handwriting.

4	Make absolutely sure that there are no errors of spelling, grammar or meaning before you send the CV to a company. Have someone else check it for you.
5	Make sure that the copy you send out is clean and not creased.
6	If you have just one master copy of your CV, keep it is a safe place (do not post it far away by accident - you will have to start again!). You can write 'MASTER' on the master with a yellow highlighting pen - the yellow will not come out on photocopies.
7	If you are sending out photocopies of your general CV, make sure that you have them made on a good machine. Many older or smaller copiers produce rather smudgy and poor copies. High Street copy shops offer the best service and their machines tend to be in perfect condition.

Always remember that your Curriculum Vitae is the brochure that is designed to sell you as a marketable product – someone who should be snapped up as a brilliant employee by the best employer. It is your first showing in the search for a job.

It must be good.

CHECKLIST TWENTY-TWO -
Dangers to avoid with CVs

Danger point – Your CV is so very important for your job hunting that you *must not make errors* in putting it together:

There are some simple rules to follow.

1	At all costs, avoid being uninteresting or boring!

2	Do not force the reader to hunt about for information. Always make your CV easy to read. Change the typeface or underline/make bold important points and headings.

3	Avoid long lists of achievements and past activities.

4	Do not 'over-produce' your CV. If you have access to something like Word on a computer, there is a temptation to make the CV too engineered, artistic and glossy. The CV must represent you perfectly - if the job is not too high-powered, then a computer-produced CV can create the wrong impression and seem more like a glossy time-share con than a straightforward statement about you, the ideal employee! Having said that, a neatly produced and presented CV from a basic WP package can look very good.

5	Do not 'over-produce' yourself either! Avoid excessive 'I was brilliant at ...' or 'My fantastic achievements were ...' Do not make extravagant claims about your skills, knowledge or successes. Do not claim to have been deeply involved in an activity when you only spent twenty minutes a week at it! Never lie about your background or working life - you will be caught out. (Remember the author's sad tale from a few pages back!)
6	If there is some slightly dubious or questionable aspect of your life or past work, then do not mention it at all unless specifically asked. (Note that some occupations may be subject to declarations about previous convictions - check the details with someone who understands the relevant law.).
7	Never allow yourself to become slipshod in your CV preparation (or in any other aspect of your job hunting, come to that!). Be a real stickler for accuracy and the perfect presentation of details and facts.

 **CHECKLIST TWENTY-THREE -
Preparing for the interview**

So, you have been invited for an interview. Well done!! At least the work you have done so far for this job has been pretty good. There are several things you must do before you turn up at the required time and place (did you remember to write confirming your attendance?)

| 1 | **Find out about the company.** This can be done in several ways - refer back to Checklist Seven - a full account is given there. |

| 2 | **Prepare yourself**

(a) **re-read the information you sent them** originally (you did keep a copy, didn't you?!) - run through the main points of your career that will probably be of special interest to them.

b) **re-read the information they sent you** - find some particular points about the company that you can ask about, such as recent success in recession or areas where they are developing new products or services.

(c) think out a few sensible and important **questions** you can ask and commit them to memory - reliable topics are:

● What are the future prospects of this job?

● What further training will be available?

● What is the company's philosophy about green issues?

<div align="right">cont.</div> |

2	**Prepare yourself** (cont)
	
	● How much will I be able to contribute to decision making in the section/department/company?
	
	● How far have they progressed with ISO9000 etc?
	
	● How does the company see itself developing over the next few years?
	
	(d) decide **what to wear** for the interview - choose an outfit that is
	
	    (i) sensible for the occasion and
	
	    (ii) represents you (you do not want to appear in an uncomfortable, starchy suit which makes you feel like a prize specimen at an exhibition!)

3	**Prepare the journey.** Be sure that you can arrive at the interview location on time. Check buses or trains, or the best route if you are driving. Plan to arrive quarter of an hour early to really check out the parking and main entrance.

Try and put yourself in the position of the recruiter – what would you be looking for in the people who are coming for interview? How would you expect them to dress for this type of job? How would you expect candidates to arrive, walk, talk, sit, converse ...? Once you have a rough idea of what you think the recruiter might want, try your best to match those supposed expectations.

If the company you are hoping to join appears from your resaearch to be fairly laid back, informal and cheerful, don't turn up dressed like a stockbroker. If the company is obviously rather old-fashioned and formal, don't turn up like an extra from a hippies' revival musical.

24 CHECKLIST TWENTY-FOUR -
Performance at the interview

This is quite a long list of things to do, once you have been invited to attend for the interview that you have been angling for all along. Before you are invited into the room, check the following points:

➢ Make sure that you have arrived well on time and at the right place.

➢ Do not come steaming in at the last minute, all hot and flustered.

➢ Make time enough to visit the loo and calm yourself before the meeting.

➢ Check that you are correctly dressed for the occasion.

➢ Take a few long, slow, deep breaths and find somewhere comfortable to wait.

➢ Switch off your mind for a moment and relax (easier said than done, but worth a try).

Once you are invited into the interview room, the whole scene changes – you are being examined as a potential employee from the very first moment.

There are a number of things that you must do.

1	**Walk tall** - appear confident (not cocky) from the beginning. Smile at the interviewer. Return any verbal greeting warmly. Never enter the room apologetically.
2	**Shake hands confidently** too. These initial greetings and pleasantries are a standard part of the interview. They allow both parties to size each other up - to make that important first impression.

3	**The first two minutes are critical.** Be careful to show that you are not fazed by the meeting, that you are there to engage in a sensible conversation between people eager to please each other. Be friendly. Be pleasant. *(It is reckoned that many interviewers **make up their minds in those two first minutes**, whether the decision is good or bad. Do not let your first few moments in the meeting cloud the issues or give false impressions about you. You must not make up your mind in those first few minutes either! If the interviewer seems rather stiff and formal, that does not mean that the whole organisation will be stiff and formal. Perhaps he or she is nervous too!)*
4	**Maintain eye-contact.** An interview is a conversation, after all, and the normal, polite courtesies should be maintained. If you keep in eye-contact with the interviewer, you will receive a clear idea of whether your answers are meeting the requirement or not. Watch the interviewer's face too and you will see nods of encouragement or scowls of displeasure. Act accordingly.
5	**Answer questions fully and clearly.** The interviewer will want answers from you - do not clam up or mumble. If you do not know the answer, say so clearly and ask for clarification. Unless you are being asked to confirm simple facts, try to avoid saying just 'yes' or 'no'. Add detail to your answer. Try to steer the conversation your way.
6	**Do not ramble on.** Make your answers comprehensive, but try not to repeat yourself or get into long descriptive narratives when a short response will do just as well.
7	**Do not lie.** Interviewers have an uncanny knack for recognising lies and deceits. You will be caught out and very likely the interview will stop then and there. In any case, you will find it difficult to sustain a lie throughout the conversation. Major on your actual achievements rather than inventing successes and experiences.

8	**Be prepared for the unusual question**. Some interviewers try to catch their candidates out by asking questions that are off the general track to see what reaction they get. Do not be bamboozled by this - stay calm and ask what the purpose of the question is.
9	**Stay alert** throughout the interview. You must maintain your attention to every word the interviewer says so that you can make the necessary replies and comments. If there is a panel of interviewers, then this is even more important. Try to make eye-contact with them all as the meeting proceeds.
10	Ask a couple of good **questions** when offered the opportunity (refer back to Checklist 23 item 2(c)). Do not ask piddling little questions like where will you sit or how long the tea break is - make the questions show that you have thought the matter through properly.
11	**Opt out if the going gets too tough**. If you realise that this really is not the job for you, for whatever reason, ask for the interview to be stopped there - this will save your time and embarrassment and the interviewer's time.
12	**Remember the social niceties**. The impression you give about your personality and your employment suitability will be helped if you follow the acceptable rules of conversation between relative strangers. • Never be rude or aggressive. • Do not fawn or suck up to the interviewer. • Do not interrupt. • Smile and nod where appropriate. • Respond carefully to the twists and turns of the conversation. • Be co-operative. • Have respect for the interviewer - this may be the only one you meet for some time! • Do not antagonise. • Try not to argue.

13	**LISTEN CAREFULLY.** (Bold, in capitals and underlined!) The success of this conversation will depend a great deal on your listening carefully to the interviewer to seek out exactly what is wanted and to understand the questions and replies. Do not repeat every question but move straight into your answer - a very brief pause before speaking is okay.
14	**Do not smoke** unless invited to do so.
15	**Sit comfortably and in a relaxed manner.** It is difficult if you are tense, but try anyway. Never sit perched on the edge of your chair. Never slouch back so far you are in danger of nodding off. Remember that the clues you give about your feelings and comfort, through the position of your limbs and facial expressions, can tell a trained observer a lot about you (see the next item).
16	**Be aware of body language.** Both you and the interviewer (or panel members) will show a great deal about feelings and attention through body language. The way you sit, cross your arms in a defensive manner, lean forward or back, twist or interlace your fingers, scratch your ear, look away when answering - all these are capable of being interpreted by observers. You will need to show signs of alertness, attention, enthusiasm, competence and comfort. Use your local library to acquire a good book on body language and look at the more common signs of good and bad behaviour and attitude. It will help you to strike a more positive pose and create a more dynamic and purposeful presence.
17	**Watch!** The interviewer may be seeking an assistant, in which case it may well be someone like him or her - a junior mirror image. Try to match what you observe, without being too obvious. See how the office is organised, what the apparent style is, what the office owner's interests are.

18	**Be natural.** Try to enjoy the interview. Make the most of the situation and learn from the experience.
19	Remember that **success only arrives when you are offered the post** - not before. Never jump to conclusions about your performance or the level of acceptance that you think you have achieved.
20	Check **what is due to happen next**. You need to know the moves that are to follow, such as letters saying yes or no, dates for further interviews and so on.
21	Always **leave with a smile**, a handshake and thanks. Leave a positive image, a picture of confidence and of being a thoroughly nice person.
22	**Caution!** Remember that you may come across a really bad interviewer, one who is not skilled, not practised, and not encouraging. You will have to take the initiative and try to direct the interview so that you can make the best impression. You know what you want to get across and you will have to move the conversation around so that you can.

Don't be daunted by this list of things to remember – most of them are simply the basic rules of careful and controlled conversation. Of course, the circumstances are somewhat different from a chat down at the pub with mates, but no one succeeds in job hunting by taking a belligerent or argumentative stance.

If you really fancy working for this outfit, then take great care not to blow it at the first meeting. If you are unsuccessful at this interview, you might want to try again later for a different job. If you have been labelled as a right bolshie, then forget it. Go somewhere else and take a different tack.

Space here for notes

25 CHECKLIST TWENTY-FIVE - Some tricky interview questions

Now that you have done all the preparation for your application and the interview, with all the important information gathered together, the time has come to consider some of the rather sneaky questions that the interviewer may throw at you. There is something of a contest in an interview, with both sides striving to win – you want the job, they want a good new employee. Both sides can win, of course, but only if they choose you!

Many interviewers believe that they are the best in the field, but sadly, many are unskilled and quite poor at the job. As a result of this absence of good training, many will try to use their favourite gimmicky question or quirky little test of your personality or background. You must not let yourself be misled by these tactics, but rather you should respond as best as you can. If it is really off-the-wall, then ask why the question is relevant. Be aware though, that this might seem like you questioning their professional style or integrity.

The following questions have all been used many times by good and bad interviewers. Read them carefully and work out what sort of answer you might give. Never let yourself be stumped over a question. If it is tricky, pause for a moment before you respond. Note that all of these except 12 and 26 are open questions that demand a narrative answer, a response that is conversational and made up of sentences, rather than just a 'yes' or 'no' answer. How would you cope with these?

A selection of difficult interview questions

I   Why do you want to change jobs – what is wrong with the present one?

2   Why do you want to work here?

3   Why should I employ you?

4   Why should I employ you rather than any of the other candidates?

5   What interests you most about this post?

6   Why do you want to change your field of work?

7   What kind of experience do you have for this work?

8   What is the best work of which you are capable?

9   What would you like to be doing in two/five/ten years time?

10 How relevant is your past training and/or qualifications?

11 Why (or why not) would you like to have your boss's job?

12 Are you willing to go where the organisation sends you?

13 What kind of decisions are most difficult for you?

14 How do you feel about your progress to date?

15 How long are you planning to stay with this organisation?

16 How did you manage over hiring and firing people?

17 How have you helped profitability, efficiency or reduction of costs and waste?

18 Why are you not earning more at your age?

19 How many people have you supervised? Have they thrived under your supervision?

20 What are the reasons for your success?

21 Why were you out of work for so long?

22 Why have you changed your jobs so frequently?

23 When did you last lose your temper, and why? How did you control the situation? Did it work?

24 What do you perceive as your greatest weaknesses and strengths?

25 What are the major qualities that you have to offer?

26 Do you still want to come and work here? If so, why; if not, why not?

27 What would your referees say about you?

28 Tell me about an event that really taxed you. How did you cope?

29 What are the areas that you and your boss disagree on?

30 How would your best friend or your worst enemy describe you?

Space here for notes

26 CHECKLIST TWENTY-SIX - Collecting a personal job file database

Buy a small pack of file cards (ideal size is office standard A6, 153mm x 102mm), punch holes in them and secure them together with a string tag or a rubber band. Alternatively buy a cheap A6 notebook and number the pages.

You will need one card (or page) for each of the following items. Do not be stingy with the cards or the amount of effort you put into filling them in. The savings on time and worry on each occasion you complete an application form will repay you many times over. You will have the perfect complete file on your working life as a permanent reference. Remember that you will only have to do this once in such detail.

An example of such a card file is shown here. It is very simple to organise.

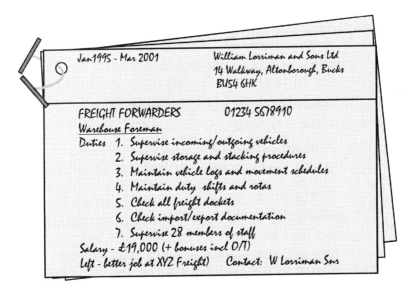

Space here for notes

Whatever happens from here
on with your job search, you
have a better chance than
most other candidates. You
have a system and a pattern
for presenting yourself in the
very best light.

SO GO ON - GET ON WITH IT!!

AND THE VERY BEST OF
LUCK!!

Useful books from Management Books 2000 Ltd

Check out our full list of books on our website –
www.mb2000.com

All About Psychological Tests and Assessment Centres by
Jack van Minden
Preparing for and passing a wide range of employment interview tests

Budget Start-ups by **Ross McBennett**
More than a hundred ways to start a business on less than £10,000

Build Your Own Rainbow by **Barrie Hopson and Mike Scally**
The definitive book for finding out what you really want to do

Careers in the City by **Joanna Minnett**
The City, financial institutions, the money markets – the jobs

Complete Entrepreneur by **David Oates**
Classic guide to entrepreneurship and making small business work

Earning a Crust by **Peter Cross**
75 interviews with women who have taken a different career path

It's All Cobblers by **Michael Carter**
The basic issues of starting a business – debunking the myths

Jobs for the Boys by **Peter Cross**
75 more interviews, with men, who have unusual jobs

Jobs, Interviews, Success by **Neil Thompson**
A career book for graduate and student job seekers

Maximise Your Potential by **Ian Seymour**
How to achieve happiness, job satisfaction, financial security

Running Your Own Business by **Robert Leach**
Comprehensive guide to setting up and running a successful business

You ... Unlimited by **A Bourne, C McCrudden and C Lyons**
Unlock the wealth in your head, do what you enjoy doing, profitably